Bugs for breakfast

Story by Annette Smith
Illustrations by Lisa Simmons

"Wake up, Mother Duck.
We are hungry,"
said Dilly Duck and Dally Duck.

Mother Duck woke up.
"We will find food for breakfast
down at the river," she said.

Mother Duck walked down the hill.

Dilly Duck and Dally Duck
ran after her.

Splash! Splash! Splash!

Mother Duck went
down into the water
to look for food.

Dilly Duck looked at a frog
sitting on a leaf.

"We can't eat frogs," he said.
"Frogs are too big
for little ducks to eat."

Dally Duck looked at the fish
swimming in the water.

"We can't eat fish," she said.
"Fish are too big
for little ducks to eat."

Dilly Duck said,
"I am very, **very** hungry."

"We can't eat frogs,
and we can't eat fish,"
said Dally Duck,
"but we **can** eat water bugs."

"We will have bugs for breakfast,"
said Dilly Duck.

"I like eating water bugs,"
said Dally Duck.

"You are **clever** little ducks,"

said Mother Duck.